The Power of Unity

Confronting Conflict in Church Leadership Teams

Lisa Lee Williams

ROYSTON
Publishing

BK Royston Publishing
P. O. Box 4321
Jeffersonville, IN 47131
502-802-5385
http://www.bkroystonpublishing.com
bkroystonpublishing@gmail.com

Cover Design: Elite Book Covers

ISBN-13: 978-1-951941-91-8

Printed in the United States of America

Dedication

I dedicate this book to every pastor, elder, ministry leader, emerging leader or pew member who has experienced the pain and isolation that unresolved conflict in the church has produced. It is true, hurt people, hurt people; however, scripture offers us all a path to healing and reconciliation as we grab hold of the Power of Unity that is found in our shared faith in Jesus Christ.

Acknowledgements

Very special thank you to Bishop Joseph W. Walker, III and my Mt. Zion Baptist Church Family. You were my training ground; the place that forged my faith and my leadership. Thank you for allowing me to grow where I was planted and then supporting my journey to soar.

Thank you to the Reverend Dr. F. Bruce Williams, Senior Pastor of Bates Memorial Baptist Church and Pastor Vincent E. James, Sr, Senior Pastor of Elim Baptist Church, for allowing me to serve your congregations as a leadership and congregation development consultant and Executive Pastor, respectively. Your trust and transparency during our service together has forged this work that I hope will serve other congregations and leaders throughout the faith community at large.

To all the ministry leaders, volunteers and congregants that I have had the honor of serving across the United States and internationally, I am grateful for how you received me and allowed me to work so intimately with you. I am truly thankful and humbled by your graciousness.

To Elder Renita Dixon and Rev. Dr. Sandra Wilson, for mining through these pages to help bring clarity to my thoughts for others to consume, thank you, thank you, thank you.

To my brothers (Tony and Greg), thank you for keeping me grounded in this process with your support and levity. When I would stress over edits or delays, I appreciate how you would always remind me, "Isn't this the book you've already written?" I love you for that.

To my pastoral cohort, Rev. Dr. Susan Lowe, Rev. Dr. Clarence Laney, Rev. Dr. John Stonesifer, Rev. Dr. Sandra A. Wilson, Elder Sandra Wilson and Elder Renita Dixon, thank you for staying in the fight with me to finish. I could not, and probably would not, have finished without the support and encouragement from each of you.

And finally, thank you to my publisher, Julia Royston of BK Publishing. You know how to birth the seemingly impossible out of people and I am grateful!

Table of Contents

INTRODUCTION
Leadership Team Conflict: A Big Problem

I have had the opportunity to meet and work many senior pastors and church leaders who characterize the leadership team at their church like this, "Individually the leaders are loyal to me. They are skilled in executing ministry programs, but they struggle to get along with one another." Does this sound familiar? How about this: is there evidence of low morale within your leadership team? Is there an unwillingness to engage with one another, or a general lack of excitement about their daily work of ministry? For those churches that are privileged to have a staff, consider this example. Do leaders with offices across the hall from one another choose to email or text their teammate to avoid face-to-face interaction? When there is face to face interaction, is it all business or worse yet, is there a notable tension in the conversation? Are the office hours becoming shorter without notification or accountability of time? Are the leadership team meetings garnering very little conversation or let alone collaboration beyond reporting on the pressing tasks at hand? Has accountability, both being held accountable and being accountable to the team, become a constant frustration? These issues may not be presenting a noticeable impact on the execution of ministry programs since things are getting done; so far as the congregants are concerned, they are getting done well. However, these are the internal dynamics of the team that reveal a breakdown in the spirit of unity that should be reflected in a Christian leadership environment. If you are concerned with conflict that is negatively impacting Christian unity within the leadership team of your church, then this book is for you.

The Role of Team Leadership

One important role of the senior pastor is to build and nurture a team of leaders who are equipped and empowered to share in the pastoral responsibilities of the church. Any pastor in this day and age would be hard-pressed to hold to the single-leader group model where the senior pastor has the sole——responsibility for determining the congregation's purpose, making all key decisions, specifying what each member needs to contribute to the church's work, setting up and overseeing communication, and measuring the success of the member's efforts while at the same time building a culture of unity.[1] Research conducted by Nancy Ammerman found that:

> [c]ongregations need people with leadership skills. They need someone who can envision what should be done and motivate others to participate in doing it. They need people who can help a group make a decision. They need people who can keep hundreds of details in order in the process of getting a large job done. They need people with whom members can identify, establishing an emotional connection that helps to bind them together as a congregation. They need people who make them feel both that things are under control at the same time that everyone has a say.[2]

The above leadership skills offered by Ammerman are necessary for the church to function efficiently.

---

[1] Kevin E. Lawson and Orbelina Eguizabal, "Leading Ministry Teams, Part II: Research on Effective Teams with Implications for Ministry Team Leadership," Christian Education Journal, 6, no. 2 (Fall 2009), 272.

[2] Nancy T. Ammerman et al., Studying Congregations: A New Handbook (Nashville, TN: Abingdon Press, 1998), 178.

However, there is one leadership characteristic that is a core value for unity in the leadership team, and that is the ability of the team members to "identify with and establish an emotional bond with members in order to bind them together as a congregation."[3] Unlike leadership in corporate organizations, the practice of Christian leadership is inextricably a shared endeavor in which each leader is expected to work with other followers of Jesus Christ as a witness to their shared faith and as an ethical commitment to operate as one body jointly knit together (Eph. 4:16).[4] This duality of collaboration and conviction goes beyond task performance directly to a reflection of the nature of God working

---

[3] Ammerman, 178.

[4] Scripture quotations are from the New Revised Standard Version Bible.

in and through the person leading. However, it is difficult to bring together individuals with varied gifts, experiences, and maturity levels and just expect them to know how to work as a team reflective of Christian unity. So as one would suspect, because of the frailties of human nature, conflict is inevitable. Therefore, attending to conflict and its causes is an ongoing work of pastoral theological reflection, and pastoral praxis that seeks is to discover and resolve the conflicts that inevitably occur in the human systems, specifically within the leadership of the church.

CHAPTER ONE

The Leadership Team: A Biblical Model of Shared Leadership

The leadership team of the church represents a model of shared leadership rooted in Biblical and theological understandings of Christian unity. When the leadership team works together in the spirit of Christian unity, they become a witness to a shared belief. The belief in the Christ event (life, death, burial, resurrection, and ultimate return of Jesus the Christ) is a unifying act of reconciliation of humanity to God, to nature, and one another. Then the perceptions and practices of leadership reflect an obligation to the same.[5] From this worldview, the leadership team is ethically compelled in everything

---

[5] Jurgen Moltmann, *The Way of Jesus Christ* (Minneapolis: Fortress Press, 1993), 214.

they do, be it ministry practices, organizational processes, and interpersonal relationships, to" make every effort to maintain the unity of the Spirit in the bond of peace." (Eph. 4:3).

The pastor, in his or her role as a visionary leader, is the primary model of practicing Christian unity for the leadership team. Psychologist Daniel Goleman, a co-author of *Primal Leadership*, defines visionary leadership as "characterized by a leader that inspires, beliefs in his or her own vision, is empathetic and explains how and why people's efforts contribute to the dream."[6] This definition also assumes a depth in the role of a pastor that goes beyond simply discerning a visionary direction for unity and sharing it with others to fulfill. It requires

---

[6] Goleman, *Primal Leadership*, 55.

the visionary leader to be engaged in the process of obtaining and maintaining unity. It requires courageous leadership that pursues leadership team unity at all costs, even in the seemingly hopeless state of leadership team conflict, and holds to "a chance for conversion – a chance for people to believe that there is hope for the future and a meaning to struggle."[7] When principles of Christian unity are both modeled and taught by the visionary leader, it passes on its characteristics to leadership team members.

Intentional education that models, trains, coaches, evaluates, and corrects in order to maintain alignment with Biblical unity is crucial to the health and witness of the leadership team.

---

[7] West, 18.

Here is a word of caution for the visionary leader. A pastor, in his or her zeal to accomplish the tasks of ministry, may unintentionally drift toward using the leadership team transactionally. This is experienced by team members when program productivity is prioritized over the personhood of those who lead. In this environment, the leadership team unity is at stake because prioritizing productivity encourages competition, and competition leads to conflict. In an environment where competition is fostered, the leadership team, just like society, will often ascribe greater value to those who are the most charismatic and influential among them. Team unity is challenged when a single person is viewed as a "rock-star."

This rock-star represents the defining perspective of much of contemporary strategy [in which] leadership [is seen] as a noun. In this perspective, the focus is on the person of the leader. Unwittingly, we have equated leadership with power [in these cases]. The function of a leader is [then diminished] to acquiring and exercising power by any means necessary – leveraging position, using coercion, playing political hardball, or outworking everyone else. When exercising power is the central value of leadership, the questions revolve around who is in charge and who makes the decisions. People defer responsibility to the [charismatic] leader, who then becomes in charge of everything. When leadership is defined by power [whether in the pastor or a leadership team member], the people [be it team members or congregants] are not mobilized for action. More often, they are listless, fearful, or simply uninvolved.[8]

This type of elitism is countercultural to Christian unity ascribed to the body of Christ. Though this can be an unintentional byproduct of a well-respected pastor or leadership team member, it ought to be confronted wherever, and in whomever, it exists.

---

[8] Ford, 129.

Such team members should be challenged to move toward a model of unity that affirms Ephesians 4:1-6

> ...lead a life worthy of the calling to which you have been called, with all humility and gentleness, with patience, bearing with one another in love, making every effort to maintain the unity of the Spirit in the bond of peace. There is one body and one Spirit, just as you were called to the one hope of your calling, one Lord, one faith, one baptism, one God and Father of all, who is above all and through all and in all.

Without a shift in thought and practice regarding the "rock-stars" among us, some "rock-stars" may begin to close ranks, exclude others, and become an exclusive subset of the leadership team in order to maintain power and influence. They may resort to withholding information, ministry expertise, and cooperation under the guise of maintaining a ministry of excellence in order to justify exclusion. The longer elite subgroups can function unchallenged, the more power and influence they gain, and the wider the bridge to team unity becomes.

CHAPTER TWO

Encouraging the Leadership Team to Lead

Larry Osborne, in his book, *Sticky Teams: Keeping Your Leadership Team and Staff on the Same Page*, recommends empowering leadership teams to lead. He makes the point that

> ...it's important that leadership team members think of themselves as leaders, not representatives. Representatives are more likely to see themselves as lobbyists for a specific constituency. Representative-oriented teams also have a harder time reaching consensus, [a byproduct of unity], when faced with a controversial issue. Leadership oriented team members... need the ability to think in terms of leading the congregation where God wants it to go. And that mindset is very different from worrying about every minority opinion or asking for an opinion poll on the front end of every significant decision. The primary job is to listen to, discern, and carry out God's will, not [the individual ministry department's or] the congregation's. This means that the leadership team is able to "make tough

decisions and move on, even if that means losing a few people who don't agree.[9]

The visionary leader should model and express empathy toward those struggling to obtain and maintain unity. Leaders do not isolate individuals from team participation or belittle the interpersonal struggle. On the contrary, empathy is the method used to bring about reconciliation, with team unity being the goal. To be empathetic "means taking [others] feelings into thoughtful consideration and then making intelligent decisions that work those feelings into the response. And, most crucially, "empathy makes resonance possible."[10] Resonance is a gift to the leadership team because it promotes

---

[9] Larry Osborne, *Sticky Teams: Keeping Your Leadership Team and Staff on the Same Page* (Grand Rapids, MI: Zondervan, 2010), 51-53.

[10] Goleman, *Primal Leadership*, 50.

the voice of others in the pursuit of unity and shows the pastor understands that maintaining unity is not a solitary work. When the leadership team is empowered and expected to participate in the work of building team unity, this is when they become true leaders and not merely program managers. Empathy and resonance are particularly important when you consider how team diversity impacts the leadership team.

The leadership team should reflect the diversity of the body of Christ if it is to be an authentic witness of unity to the congregation and the world. When it does not reflect the community of believers, the witness of the team is marred with inconsistency when the voices, gifts, and passions of all of God's people, particularly women, are excluded. When women are represented in the leadership team of the church, Christian unity allows

her voice, her motivation, and her integrity to be

maintained and not challenge even when she stands

in opposition to the status quo. The reality is that

women experience the subtleties of systemic

marginalization and silencing (even in the church)

when they take the courage to "deliver disturbing

news and raise difficult questions in a way that

people can absorb, prodding them to take up the

message [and act]."[11] The leadership team must

sensitize its unity lens to address practices of

silencing, dismissing, or excluding marginalized

groups, such as women, from full engagement in the

---

[11] Ronald A. Heifetz et al., *Leadership on the Line: Staying Alive Through the Dangers of Leading* (Boston, MA: Harvard School Press, 2002), 12.

leadership of the church, if authentic Christian unity is to be realized.

Moreover, the Barna Report entitled *20 Years of Surveys Show Key Differences in the Faith of America's Men and Women* and published August 1, 2011, shows statistically that "[w]omen have traditionally been the backbone of volunteer activity in churches. However, there has been a nine-point slide in the percentage of women helping out at a church during any given week. That drop reflects a 31% reduction in the non-paid female workforce at churches."[12] For ordained women, "reasons for leaving the ministry include lack of support from the hierarchical system... [that result[s] in them hitting

---

[12] The Barna Report, Barna.com, accessed February 1, 2016, http://www.barna.com/research/20-years-of-surveys-show-key-differences-in-the-faith-of-americas-men-and-women/.

the] "stained-glass ceiling" when it comes to succeeding in the male-dominated ministry."[13] Even with that decline, women still outnumber men in the daily work of ministry. According to the same Barna Report, "[t]he percentage of men who volunteer at a church during a typical week has slipped by six percentage points since 1991 to its present level of 18%."[14] Though women systematically experience more difficulty in a male-dominated hierarchal structure as found in many churches, it is only fair to say "when [anyone] exercise[s] leadership [he or she] risk[s] getting marginalized, diverted, attacked, or seduced."[15] For leadership teams to maintain unity

---

[13] Susan Willhauck and Jacquelyn Thorpe, *The Web of Women's Leadership: Recasting Congregational Ministry* (Nashville, TN: Abingdon Press, 2001), 23.

[14] The Barna Report

[15] Heifetz, *Leadership on the Line*, 31.

with a diverse group, they ought to have leaders who exercise great empathy and understanding in this decline in church involvement because women and men are leaving the church—leaders and non-leaders alike.

Waiting on the Team to Mature

The pastor and team leaders can be courageous in managing the frustrating tension that arises when waiting for people to mature to the place of consistent practices of unity. For the church organization that operates through a model of team leadership, involves both full-time and volunteer leaders, it ought to remember that for the most part, "[t]he church is voluntary in the sense that people choose to belong or not, and usually work together without the restraints found in business organizations where people do what the boss says or get fired."[16]

The pastor should be aware that even those who take a paid position of leadership in the church and do so out of a sense of personal call or passion; when confronted with conflict, they are still subject to the fear of rejection and exclusion experienced in the marketplace such as 'what will happen if my work or I am deemed inadequate?' They may become afraid of being fired. As a result, they may fight, control, and coerce in order to maintain their paycheck or save face versus working to resolve interpersonal or performance issues that are resulting in conflict. Managing these tensions in the life of the leadership

---

[16] David Sawyer, *The Work of the Church: Getting the Job Done in Boards and Committees* (Pressia, PA: Judson Press, 1987), 8.

team is a pastoral responsibility and a very important one.

CHAPTER THREE

Team Unity as a Witness of Faith

What a leadership team believes about unity and the love ethic required for maintaining it is reflected in how leaders experience harmony and prioritize the management and maintenance of interpersonal relationships within the church. Unity matters because it is central to God's plan to unite all things in Christ. As such, it reflects the very nature of God, the church, and the faith of those who believe in the reconciling power of Jesus Christ. To maintain and nurture unity in a team leadership environment, it is necessary to confront gaps in belief and ministry practices that conflict can create (whether explicit or implicit).

The Love Ethic of Unity

The leadership team, as a representation of the mystical body of Christ, is infused with the nature of God through one Spirit indwelling in her members as love. The spiritually mature team embodies the "Holy Spirit [as] love personified, the product of the mutual love of the Father and the Son, the life-principle of the Church [which] can be equally well described as [a union of] love."[17] Paul illustrates this embodied love in practice in 1 Corinthians 13:2, 4-8a when he writes,

> [I]f I have prophetic powers and understand all mysteries and all knowledge, and if I have all faith, so as to remove mountains, but do not have love, I am nothing...Love is patient; love is kind; love is not envious or boastful or arrogant or rude. It does not insist on its own way; it is not irritable or resentful; it does not

---

[17] Kelly, 414.

rejoice in wrongdoing but rejoices in the truth. It bears all things, believes all things, hopes all things, endures all things. Love never ends.

Love maintains unity, and unity is an expression of Christian love in practice.

In Ephesians chapter two, the apostle Paul also associates the essence of love expressed in the mystical body with faith and hope as a natural combination. By grounding love in faith and hope, the leadership team is then able to locate itself in the spectrum of the life of the church from faith believing inclusion ("by grace you have been saved through faith" Eph. 2:8) to eternal redemption ("and raised us up with Him and seated us with Him in heavenly places in Christ Jesus" Eph. 2:6). Faith and hope inspire humility in service unto God in relationship with others when challenges to unity arise. This way of understanding God's creation and desired engagement with the leadership team produces a unity culture in which all leaders subject their will and perspectives about relationships and practices to the headship and worldview of Jesus Christ as revealed through scripture.

Grace and Unity

What the leadership team believes about grace and Christian unity directly impacts how members conduct themselves with one another. Grace is the love and mercy given to us by God because God desires us to have it, not necessarily because of anything we have done to earn it. The leadership team identity is forged through the interplay of belief between expressing grace to one another and the love ethic of the community. Amy

Plantinga Pauw, in her essay "Attending to the Gaps Between Belief and Practices," states that beliefs are what make "practices intentional as opposed to random or reflexive" actions; [therefore,] struggles persist in maintaining unity when there are gaps between beliefs and practices."[18] When attending to the gap between unifying beliefs about grace and expressions of love, Augustine suggests "the antithesis of love is the spirit that promotes schisms, rendering Christ's seamless robe and tearing His body apart."[19] These divisions among team members, in all their forms, are conflicts that corrupt the body of Christ and results in self-isolation that

---

[18] Amy Plantinga Pauw, "Attending to the Gaps Between Belief and Practices," *Practicing Theology: Beliefs and Practices in Christian Ministry*, ed. Miroslav Volf and Dorothy C. Bass (Grand Rapids, MI: Wm. B. Eerdmans Publishing Co., 2002), 34.

[19] Kelly, 414.

destroys team unity. Jürgen Moltmann says, "[t]he isolated individual is the perversion of what a person is. If people are to be able to live as persons, body and soul, they must discover the Divine dignity of community and look for the future of community; it is only in sociality that personhood can be developed if it is not to be perverted into egotistical individualism."[20] It might be easy to gloss over this assertion and think that if a person is egotistical and works in isolation, it is somehow that person's choice. The perspective being offered here is that self-isolation is a byproduct of gaps between the leadership teams' beliefs about maintaining Christian unity through grace and love. Attending to the gap with intentional discipleship and practice

---

[20] Moltmann, 267

allows all members of the leadership team the grace

to stay fully engaged.

CHAPTER FOUR

Moving from Performance to the Practice of Unity

Though leaders can successfully conduct liturgies and programs that emphasize the unifying power of Jesus Christ, "[t]rue belief and good results are not sufficient conditions for excellent practice."[21] It is the attitude that one holds amid ministry service and the character that one displays that is the more excellent way. Again, there is this correlation between love and ministry practice that suggests it is not enough for the leadership team to believe well and practice well. It must also love well. It is a profound statement to say, "even if there is excellence in ministry practice, if there is no love, there is no unity." This view boldly confronts all the

---

[21] Pauw, 39.

cultural ideology that has crept into church leadership today that implies, "I don't have to like you to work with you." But if the gap between our unifying beliefs and our leadership practice of grace and love is truly challenged, that sentiment is turned on edge with a response that says, "No! You have to love me to work with me, or our work is in vain."

Why is this distinction so important to make? When a person holds the belief that the nature of God is loving and reconciling, but he or she resists maintaining a loving, reconciled relationship with others, a "war between beliefs and practices" disfigures that person's actions.[22] The truth of the belief about the nature of God remains true whether one acts on it or not, but the practice of the one who

---

[22] Pauw, 39.

resists accepting this nature of God for him or herself sets their personal desire against the theological truth they profess to believe. Pauw says these "weakly held or inconsistent beliefs are a barrier to good practice, but more impactful is the failure "to desire the right things."[23] The longer this war between belief and behavior is allowed to remain unaddressed in the life of the leadership team, the more conflict will abound and become a cultural norm. However, shared beliefs conveyed in love provide a space of grace in which the team can reconcile any gaps between belief and practice that allows an opportunity to mature and grow in harmony together. Without grace as a way of engaging in team leadership, the team may unintentionally adopt a

---

[23] Pauw, 45.

works ethic that believes God will reward or judge eternal salvation based on the effectiveness or ineffectiveness of one's personal actions.

Serene Jones, in her article "Graced Practices: Excellence and Freedom in Christian Life," rejects a "works righteousness" because it "limits the extent and efficacy of God's grace" and does not take into account "the reconciling grace in Jesus Christ."[24] As leaders, the ability to personally embrace a grace ethic that is applied both to oneself and is extended to others allows for the freedom to practice ministry with others without fear of condemnation from within the team. Failures in

---

[24] Serene Jones, "Graced Practices: Excellence and Freedom in Christian Life," *Practicing Theology: Beliefs and Practices in Christian Life,* ed. Miroslav Volf and Dorothy C. Bass (Grand Rapids, MI: Wm. B. Eerdmans Publishing Co., 2002), 515.

personal character, lack of doctrinal proficiency, or

productivity measures are overcome by extending

grace as an expression of the unifying power of

God's love. Grace assumes, first and foremost, that

"Christian practice is a response, always inadequate,

to merciful divine presence; it does not establish the

truth of this presence."[25] Even when the leader

believes that grace is a gift freely given from God and

chooses, for whatever reason, not to embrace it in

practice, grace is still a free gift from God and ought

to be reflected in the shared belief and practices of

team leadership in the Church.

This relationship between belief and practice

asserts, "[p]ractices are not just things we do in light

of doctrine; practices are what we become as we are

---

[25] Pauw, 36.

set in motion in the space of doctrine."[26] This notion of becoming reaches back to the love and grace ethic and reinforces the role of shared belief in team leadership formation. Whether led by the pastor or members of the leadership team, ongoing team development in the area of Christian unity brings about the stability and continuity that narrows the gap between beliefs and practices within leadership teams. Ministry practices are then influenced by this shared study, resulting in a leadership team with the Biblical and theological foundation necessary to confront conflict while maintaining a commitment to work together in the union of love.

---

[26] Jones, 75.

CHAPTER FIVE

The Human Factor: Understanding Family Systems

Building healthy teams is not merely an act of Biblical and theological reflection. It also involves the relational work of understanding human systems theory. Because people are involved, it's not an easy undertaking even for the most faithful and committed among us.

Ronald Richardson, in his book *Creating a Healthier Church: Family Systems Theory, Leadership, and Congregational Life*, explains why interpersonal relationships in teams are so difficult to navigate. He says that "[e]very act of ministry, exercise of leadership, or way of relating to others in the church comes from an underlying belief, or theory, about how human beings' function."[27] He

goes on to say that

> [n]o one lives or acts in isolation, and we are
> all affected by each other's behavior.
> Verbally individuals can profess the same
> faith but behaviorally have significantly
> different faiths. They can get caught up in an
> emotional process that impedes their ability
> to express their faith behaviorally. Faith and
> practice come closer together when
> leadership is expressed more effectively, and
> ministry is engaged in because of a sense of
> connection and shared responsibility. When
> faith and practice are more closely aligned in
> the environment, no one feels accused or
> attacked or put down or needs to evade his or
> her own responsibility. And no one is singled
> out as "the problem" or the only one who
> should take responsibility.[28]

The alignment of belief and practice within the

community of faith should result in the following:

---

[27] Ronald W. Richardson, *Creating a Healthier
Church: Family Systems, Leadership, and Congregational
Life* (Minneapolis, MN: Fortress Press, 1996), 24.

[28] Richardson, 26.

individuals take responsibility for their own part and yet function cooperatively in relations with others. Each one can give and take guidance, teach, and learn from one another resulting in a balance of individual responsibility and community awareness, concern, and connection.[29] In this type of environment, teams fulfill unity in a more focused and unified manner.

However, when leadership teams focus on their problems, attention is taken away from maintaining unity. This is not to say that the leadership team will not have "times of imbalance in the [team's] emotional system, times when there are conflicts and problems that challenge leadership unity…but how the situation turns out…depends

---

[29] Richardson, 26.

primarily on the actions and reactions of the church leadership."[30] As Richardson says above, it is the emotional system that can cause a group or individual to be unable or unwilling to express unity behaviorally, which can, in turn, ruin the efforts of team leadership in other areas of ministry mission as well. Attending to the health of the leadership team's emotional system is not the responsibility of an individual, but rather the work of the entire team. Those who share in leadership should be aware of how the emotional system operates within the team and how it impacts Christian unity within the team and the church at large. Most importantly, leaders need "to be aware of the part they play in the emotional system and how they can become a more

---

[30] Richardson, 30.

constructive force for improving the emotional life of the church.[31]

---

[31] Richardson, 29.

CHAPTER SIX

Emotional Intelligence and Team Dynamics

Building an emotionally healthy leadership team requires each member to grow in emotional intelligence. Based on Daniel Goleman's article in the *Harvard Business Review*, "What Makes a Leader?" he provides guidelines on what it means to be an emotionally intelligent leader. These are leaders who are self-aware, meaning they have:

...the ability to recognize and understand their moods, emotions, drives, as well as their effect on others. Emotionally intelligent leaders are able to self-regulate by controlling and redirecting disruptive impulses and moods. They have the ability to suspend judgment - to think before acting. This leader is also self-motivated with a passion to work for reasons that go beyond money or status and have the propensity to pursue goals with energy and persistence." This leader also expresses empathy toward others and has the ability to understand the emotional makeup of other people and has the skill to treat people according to their emotional reactions. And finally, the emotionally intelligent leader possesses social skills that allow him or her to be "proficient in managing relationships and building networks that include finding common ground and building rapport."[32]

These are traits that are beneficial at all levels of leadership within the church. The leadership team should commit to embracing these personal characteristics as a standard for leadership recruitment and practice. In doing so, the leadership team will be more emotionally healthy, and the experience of Christian unity will be more authentic. This shift toward expecting and nurturing emotional intelligence within the leadership team may result in congregants, who have retreated to the pews, to hear and respond to a call to serve because the emotional

---

[32] Daniel Goleman, "What Makes a Leader," 95-96.

intelligence of the leadership is no longer a barrier to ministry involvement.

There are challenges as well as opportunities associated with building healthy leadership teams. M. Scott Peck, in his book *The Different Drum: Community Making and Peace*, rightly highlights for us that people have to want to be in a community.[33] The leadership team has to want to have intimate relationships with the people they serve and worship with every week. Whether it is the person who serves in pastoral leadership, works on the staff, volunteers in a ministry, or a member of the congregation in general, people have to be willing to resolve any "emotional baggage" that becomes a barrier to

---

[33] M. Scott Peck, The Different Drum: Community Making and Peace. (New York: Simon & Schuster, 1987), audiobook.

moving into the stages of a community (or Christian unity) making. Peck offers four dynamic stages of community formation, and he cautions that the community can move in and out of any stage at any time. These stages are pseudo-community, chaos, emptiness, and community.[34]

Be aware that highly functioning leadership teams can appear to be an authentic community. In actuality, they may live somewhere between a "pseudo-community" where everyone is nice, polite, avoids conflict, and withholds truth for the sake of getting the ministry events done, and "chaos" in which the differences are no longer tolerable and conflict erupts. This vacillation between these two stages keeps the leadership team stuck just short of

---

[34] M. Scott Peck, Audiobook.

an authentic, intimate community reflective of unity and love. Leadership teams who are exhibiting signs of moving back and forth between pseudo-community and conflict could benefit from some affiliative style leadership from the visionary leader. The affiliative leadership style "creates harmony by connecting people to each other to heal rifts in a team, [provide motivation] during stressful times, [and] strengthen connections."[35] Through this leadership technique, the visionary leader can assist in moving through the stage of chaos into the stage of emptiness. Here, the team can choose to remove the barriers, expectations, and judgments that hinder their ability to acknowledge and embrace their

---

[35] Daniel Goleman, Primal Leadership: Unleashing the Power of Emotional Intelligence (Boston MA: Harvard Business Review Press, 2013), Kindle edition.

differences for the sake of unity. The team must go through the stages of pseudo-community, chaos, and emptiness for authentic unity to be established. Otherwise, disunity will always exist (even silently) in the leadership culture. Where there is disunity, there is no real community.

Building the emotional intelligence of the leadership team also requires establishing "rules of engagement" that involve "[d]iscovering the emotional reality, visualizing the ideal, and sustaining emotional intelligence" in practice.[36] The goal is to

> ...involve people in discovering the truth about themselves and the organization. [To help the team] recognize the truth about what is *really* going on and help people to name what is harmful and to build on the

---

[36] Goleman, *Primal Leadership*, 218.

[leadership team's] strengths. At the same time, bring people together around a dream of what could be, and in the process, create and demonstrate new ways for people to work together.[37]

The leadership team that is event focused can fall into the trap of valuing individual productivity versus the value of maintaining Christian unity that comes from working together. The pursuit of individual ministry goals puts team members in competition with one another. Since competition is antithetical to collaboration, conflict ultimately arises as individual leaders vie for space, resources, and time on the church calendar. This focus on "me" versus "we" becomes exaggerated in the emotional system of the leadership team. For example, when members of the leadership team are confronted with a problem or a

---

[37] Goleman, *Primal Leadership*, 218.

criticism, "[i]f the leaders [of the team] think in individualistic terms they are likely to respond to attacks as though they personally were being attacked (what they hear), rather than seeing the attack as part of an imbalance in the system. If they think this way, however they respond, whatever they actually do or say, more problems will result, and [the team relationships] will become more chaotic."[38]   Moreover, if the leaders think in individualistic terms, the way that problems and criticisms are represented to others, the story they tell will convey the sentiments of a personal attack. At this point, the accuser excuses himself or herself from any responsibility for the causes or resolution of the problem at hand.

---

[38] Richardson, 30.

CHAPTER SEVEN

High Performing Teams and Conflict Avoidance

Sometimes because the outcomes of the leadership team effort are producing great ministry programming, the tendency is to delay or disengage from resolving issues when they arise. This practice of conflict avoidance fails to confront the motives of leadership conflict by asking the question, "What do the leaders have that they don't want to give up?" It would be easy to compile a list of sinister self-serving motives, but more often than not, the fear of conflict is simply a fear of change. In essence, a fear of changing self and a fear of change in the environment.

> [Leaders] resist change for one reason: it is painful. And most church leaders don't know what to do with that reality. If preaching about it doesn't work, the tendency is to

preach about it more. If confronting the dissenters has not been effective, confront more. If people resist unilateral decisions, why not become more autocratic? More of the same never works. By failing to come to grips with how cultural dysfunctions deeply impact the health of the church, our leaders will continue to fail to discern an essential reality concerning the nature of change: *Culture shapes churches, and churches shape people – often through the power of what remains unspoken.*[39]

In that unspoken realm is the reality that leaders typically don't want to look at themselves as being weak or dominated by others. Consequently, they resist being vulnerable enough to engage challenges and conflict from an emotionally healthy space. Some choose to entrench themselves in a perspective or position that isolates them from the team or particular people. For example, Barry Oshry, in his book, *Seeing Systems: Unlocking the Mysteries of*

---

[39] Ford, 39.

Organizational Life, says when leaders are involved in "turf warfare", 'this is less likely to be a personal issue – much as it may seem like that to the participants – than a systemic one, a vulnerability that develops with remarkable regularity in the [leadership] world; therefore, to deal with a turf issue as a personal issue is to miss the point entirely. This is true of many other "personal" issues in organizational life as well.'[40]

> When we don't see systems, we fall out of the possibility of partnership with one another; we misunderstand one another; we make up stories about one another; we have our myths and prejudices about one another; we hurt and destroy one another; we become antagonists when we could be friends; we oppress one another when we could live in peace; and our systems – organizations, families, task forces, faith groups, [leadership teams] – squander much of their potential.

---

[40] Oshry, Kindle loc 236 of 3895.

All of this happens without awareness or choice.[41]

Barry Oshry asserts that "how such thinking is the costly illusion of system blindness – an illusion that results in needless stress, destructive conflicts, broken relationships, missed opportunities, and diminished [team] effectiveness."[42] Systems blindness is equivalent to the parable in Matthew 7:1-5 that cautions Christians to be careful in their judgment of others since our integrity is challenged when we presume to rightly see the speck in our neighbor's eye but cannot see the log in our own eye. Oshry reminds us that "the most dangerous thing about blindness is that when we're blind, we don't

---

[41] Oshry, Kindle loc 252 of 3895.

[42] Oshry, Kindle loc 236 of 3895

know we're blind. We think we can see. We take what we see as the truth, and we act."[43]

The leadership team must practice empathy and grace in navigating systems blindness. By doing so, the team develops the ability to see how each member at any given time can take an action that "leads the team out of the possibilities of partnership and into relationships of opposition, antagonism, disappointment, and warfare."[44] In order to move toward authentic unity in light of these systemic dynamics, there must exist a "joint commitment to the success of whatever endeavor, process, or project the team is engaged in that recognizes the dance of systems blindness that has the potential to impede

---

[43] Oshry, 55.

[44] Oshry, 61.

that success."[45] How leaders take responsibility for the emotional system of the leadership team is the work of developing the emotional intelligence of the group. The result is a leadership community of trust and unity that is sustainable when conflict happens, as it inevitably will.

---

[45] Oshry, 85.

CHAPTER EIGHT

Strategies for Team Assessment

One church sociologist observes: "[a] crucial task for pastoral leaders and a key first step in practical theological thinking is helping [the pastor as team leader] gain a realistic picture of [his or her team], its situation, and its possibilities in the present and immediate future."[46] To discover what is going on in a particular context, Nancy Ammerman, in her book *Studying Congregations*, suggests using an ethnographic research approach utilizing a needs assessment tool to accomplish the pastoral theological praxis of discovery. The purpose of a needs assessment is to gather information necessary to understand how the leadership team comprehends,

---

[46] Ammerman, 173.

interprets, and measures the various aspects of team function, and to expose and examine the interactions that link "behavior with beliefs and values with actions" in this case, as it relates to maintaining Christian unity. [47] The use of a needs assessment survey is not intended to be a reactive response to leadership team issues, but rather to "enable [the pastor] to understand more fully how [he or she] can legitimately meet the spiritual and relational needs of the team."

Jackson W. Carroll is the contributing writer of Chapter 6 in *Studying Congregations,* and he addresses "Leadership and the Study of the Congregation." He writes:

Without such realistic assessments, whether general or specific, [pastors] often experience

---

[47] Ammerman, 105.

frustration. Either they fail to see new possibilities...because of an inadequate grasp of the situation, or they find that their dreams for the future do not fit the realities of the situation. They are blocked by "mental models" – images or assumptions, often untested, about the ways things are – that do not fit the situation...[O]ur mental models often hold us captive to old ways of thinking and acting that have no relevance to the present circumstances. Often, too, our mental models reflect what are called "cohort" or generational differences in perspectives, perspectives shaped by experiences during the years in which a generation came of age. A problem with mental models...is that they are often tacit. They exist below the level of awareness. Thus, if [pastors] are to help [their leadership teams] make a realistic assessment of [their] situation, [they] will need to help [team members] become aware of their models, their assumptions about the way things are.[48]

Discovering the mental models of the leadership team by assessing leadership perceptions

----

[48] Ammerman, 174.

"…involves both inquiry–surfacing relevant data regarding the issue under consideration–and reflection–asking how the data confirms or challenges or corrects existing mental models."[49] As churches grow and change over the years, new leaders come and go. The result is often a generational gap in expectations for leadership team members. For example, those who were leaders in the early stages of the church's development when the congregation was smaller, the budget was lower, and responsibilities of leadership were more autonomous, perhaps out of necessity, may now find it difficult to be accountable to other team leaders for what they do in their ministries. New leaders brought on board later in the church's development may find

---

[49] Ammerman, 174.

it difficult to understand why other leaders are not more collaborative or open to suggestions and change. When pastoral leadership understands how mental models shape leadership perceptions, he or she is able to contextualize conflict in terms of individual experience rather than assuming there is some motivation of defiance when conflict occurs.

Priestly Listening and Theology of Presence

Richard R. Osmer, in his book, *Practical Theology: An Introduction*, suggest using the Descriptive-Empirical method. 'It is the act of priestly listening that is grounded in a theology of presence that allows one to attend to others in their particularity and otherness within the presence of God.'[50] This can be accomplished as a member of

---

[50] Osmer, 33.

the team, or you can engage an outside spiritual presence to conduct the research, but the goal is the same, to offer "the quality of the attentiveness congregational leaders give to people and events in their everyday lives."[51] The key term is "attending," that is, to relate to others with openness, attentiveness, and prayerfulness. This method obligates the listener to slow down and engage the others intimately. It necessitated attending to one's personal practices and perceptions of relating to others as a leader. This method offers the opportunity to reflect on such things as: "[h]ow can [I] lead if [I] fail to attend to others in their particularity and otherness? What sort of influence do [I] have to offer if [I] have not struggled to overcome [my] own

---

[51] Osmer, 33.

tendency to not listen, to rush to judgment, and to ignore suffering others in our midst? Struggling with these kinds of issues lies at the heart of a spirituality of presence. It is a matter of opening [oneself] up to the forming and transforming Spirit of God who remakes us in the image of Christ within His body. Unless we first learn to attend, we cannot [truly] lead."[52]

The role of intercessory prayer in priestly listening requires entering into the situation of others through personal contact, listening with empathic imagination. It then moves upward to God, placing the others' needs and concerns before God in prayer on their behalf. This twofold movement reflects the

---

[52] Osmer, 34.

pattern of the priestly office of Jesus Christ."[53] While the spirituality of presence through priestly listening "involves attending to others in personal relationships, it also includes investigating the circumstances and cultural contexts of others in more formal and systematic ways."[54]

---

[53] Osmer, 35.

[54] Osmer, 37.

CHAPTER NINE

Using Teamwork Theory in Your Assessment

Consider using Patrick Lencioni's book, *The Five Dysfunctions of a Team,* to assess the leadership team's perceptions regarding barriers to team unity. He provides a framework for organizing and interpreting team dynamics leading to the disunity that include lack of trust, fear of conflict, lack of commitment, avoidance of accountability, and inattention to team goals. The first team dysfunction, lack of trust, is translated through team perceptions around team morale. Team morale is understood as "the mental and emotional condition (as of enthusiasm, confidence, or loyalty) of an individual or group with regard to the function or tasks at hand."[55] Team morale is negatively impacted when team members do not trust one another. Without trust, unity is impossible to maintain. "[T]rust is the confidence among team members that their peers' intentions are good, and that there is no reason to be protective or careful around the group."[56] Enthusiasm, confidence and loyalty to the team are forged by the team's ability to be vulnerable with one another. Lencioni avers "it requires team members to [expose themselves] to one another and be confident that their respective vulnerabilities will not be used against them. The vulnerabilities [he is] referring to include weaknesses, skill deficiencies, interpersonal

---

[55] Merriam-Webster, accessed September 24, 2017, https://www.merriam-webster.com/dictionary/morale

[56] Lencioni, 195.

shortcomings, mistakes, and requests for help."[57]

Indicators that members of a team lack trust are

> ...they conceal their weaknesses and mistakes from one another. They hesitate to ask for help or provide constructive feedback. They hesitate to offer help outside their own areas of responsibility. They jump to conclusions about the intentions and aptitudes of others without attempting to clarify them. They fail to recognize and tap into one another's skills and experiences. They waste time and energy managing their behaviors for effect. They hold grudges. They dread meetings and find reasons to avoid spending time together.[58]

Discovering how these characteristics are informing perceptions regarding team morale reveals the level of trust the team is experiencing. Additionally, how the pastor, as a team leader, engages in building trust through modeling vulnerability must also be

---

[57] Lencioni, 196.

[58] Lencioni, 197.

considered. For "[t]he most important action that a [a pastor as team leader] must take to encourage the building of trust on a team is to demonstrate vulnerability first."[59]

The second dysfunction, fear of conflict, correlates with team member perceptions regarding healthy communication within the team. Without healthy communication, conflict is avoided, and unity cannot be sustained. Lencioni asserts, "[b]y building trust, a team makes conflict possible because team members do not hesitate to engage in passionate and sometimes emotional debate, knowing that they will not be punished for saying something that might otherwise be interpreted as

---

[59] Lencioni, 201.

destructive or critical."[60] How the team perceives communication practices revealed through their willingness and ability to communicate with one another in such a way that does not undermine the foundation of trust. When making the assessment regarding communication and its role in team conflict, Lencioni reminds team leaders that

...it is important to distinguish productive ideological conflict from destructive fighting and interpersonal politics. Ideological conflict is limited to concepts and ideas, and avoids personality-focused, mean-spirited attacks. However, it can have many of the same external qualities of interpersonal conflict— passion, emotion, and frustration— so much so that an outside observer might easily mistake it for unproductive discord.[61]

---

[60] Lencioni, 202.

[61] Lencioni, 202.

As a means of interpretation, Lencioni's highlights that "teams that fear conflict . . . have boring meetings. They create environments where back-channel politics and personal attacks thrive. They ignore controversial topics that are critical to team success. They fail to tap into all the opinions and perspectives of team members. They waste time and energy with posturing and interpersonal risk management."[62] All of which are behaviors to undermine Christian unity.

Third, the lack of commitment results when team members do not have the ability to influence decisions that affect them. The goal of team commitment is not to garner consensus or certainty on every action the team needs to make, but rather to

---

[62] Lencioni, 204.

allow and encourage each team member to have input into the decisions or problems the team is addressing, which in turn supports unity. Team members who feel they have the ability to influence decisions that affect them are more likely to commit to the agreed-upon goals of the team, even when they didn't vote for the decision. The reason being, "reasonable human beings do not need to get their way to support a decision, but only need to know that their opinions have been heard and considered."[63] To assess lack of commitment within a team, Lencioni suggests

> ...a team that fails to commit . . . creates ambiguity among the team about direction and priorities. Watches windows of opportunity close due to excessive analysis and unnecessary delay. Breeds lack of confidence and fear of failure. Revisits

---

[63] Lencioni, 207.

discussions and decisions again and again. Encourages second-guessing among team members.[64]

When team members are silent in team meetings and disengage from the collaborative process of conflict resolution and problem-solving, it is an indication that the team (or a team member) is not committing to the decision at hand and has possibly slipped into self-isolation. Silence is a way of veiling one's commitment that may not be revealed until action is required. The ability for team members to commit to a specific goal is achieved only after everyone has contributed their opinion and the team leader clearly states the decision based on their efforts. Therefore, the team leader must be comfortable enough to allow and encourage each team member to participate in

---

[64] Lencioni, 209.

team decision-making for team members to believe their opinion is desired and considered. Otherwise, the perception that leaders have influence over decisions that affect them and commitment to team goals is not achieved, and yes, unity is eroded.

Fourth, the lack of commitment results in the avoidance of accountability within the team dynamic. When team members are not committed to team goals, team members often vocalize their dissatisfaction to the team leader with the expectation that the team leader should and will hold that individual accountable for their inaction. Lencioni argues, however, that accountability "refers specifically to the willingness of team members to call their peers on performance or behaviors that might hurt the team [or disrupt team unity]."[65] The team leader has the responsibility to empower the team to hold one another accountable. He or she only engages the team in this process when the team needs assistance or when removing a team member becomes necessary. A team that avoids accountability

> ...creates resentment among team members who have different standards of performance. Encourages mediocrity. Misses deadlines and key deliverables. Places an undue burden on the team leader as the sole source of discipline.[66]

Assessing the team perceptions regarding accountability and who is responsible for assuring accountability is a way to identify to what degree

---

[65] Lencioni, 212.

[66] Lencioni, 214.

team members understand the role of accountability in maintaining unity.

And finally, concerning inattention to results, Lencioni says, "[t]he ultimate dysfunction of a team is the tendency of members to care about something other than the collective goals of the group. If teammates are not being held accountable for their contributions, they will be more likely to turn their attention to their own needs, and to the advancement of themselves or their departments."[67] It is in the area of maintaining focus on results that the role of the pastor as a team leader is of utmost importance. As the visionary leader for the team, the pastor must actively and consistently keep the vision for the team at the forefront for all team members. He or she must

---

[67] Lencioni, 216.

measure the team's success based on their ability to achieve those goals as a team and nothing else. Lencioni reinforces the importance of the role of the team leader in this regard when he says:

> Perhaps more than with any of the other dysfunctions, the team leader must set the tone for a focus on results. If team members sense that the team leader values anything other than results, they will take that as permission to do the same for themselves. Team leaders must be selfless and objective, and reserve rewards and recognition for those who make real contributions to the achievement of group goals.[68]

Team members may not articulate the need for pastoral engagement in these terms. However, the level of satisfaction they hold regarding pastoral engagement with the team may be the unspoken request the pastor does not want to ignore because

---

[68] Lencioni, 219-220.

the unity of the team may very well be at stake.

CHAPTER TEN

A Biblical Strategy for Confronting Conflict

EUODIA AND SYNTYCHE: The Fight Heard
Around the World

The challenge of maintaining unity in the

body of Christ has been a concern of leadership

throughout scripture, especially in the Pauline

Epistles. The apostle Paul raises the issue of disunity

in an open letter "[t]o all the saints in Christ Jesus

who are in Philippi, with the bishops and deacons."

(Phil. 1:1). Though he was writing for multiple

reasons, one primary purpose was an exhortation to

unity in the face of opposition from those outside of

the church as well as conflict within.[69] He writes,

> If then there is any encouragement in Christ,
> any consolation from love, any sharing in the

---

[69] Katharine Doob Sakenfeld, *The New Interpreter's
Dictionary of the Bible D-H*, Vol. 2 (Nashville, TN: Abingdon
Press, 2007), 505.

Spirit, any compassion and sympathy, make my joy complete: be of the same mind, having the same love, being in full accord and of one mind. Do nothing from selfish ambition or conceit, but in humility regard others as better than yourselves. Let each of you look not to your own interests but to the interests of others. Let the same mind be in you that was in Christ Jesus. (Phil. 2:1-5)

Though this portion of the letter begins as an address to the entire community, Paul shifts his focus to the leadership and addresses the conflict between Euodia and Syntyche. (Phil. 4:2-3)

In chapter four of Philippians, Paul outlines a model for pastoral response to leaders in conflict. First, he affirms that Euodia and Syntyche share leadership with him versus work for him. Though Paul, in his pastoral and apostolic role, has different responsibilities from Euodia and Syntyche, he affirms the value of these two women as part of a team leadership structure at the church in Philippi, by acknowledging their contribution and impact as leaders who have "struggled beside [him] in the work of the gospel." (Phil. 4:3c.)

Second, Paul refers to them as his "sisters" versus daughters in ministry. Sisterhood illustrates familial equality in their relationship to God as Father and to one another in their shared leadership to the local church. This distinction between sisters versus daughters is of utmost importance. Some denominations and fellowships have adopted the perspective of a pastor as father or mother and consider those who serve in non-pastoral leadership as sons and daughters.[70] This perspective cheapens the individual call to leadership in non-pastoral

---

[70] Larry Kreider, *The Cry for Spiritual Fathers and Mothers* (Ephrata: PA: House to House Publishing, 2000)

capacities. It perverts the theological theme of co-laborers. It reinforces the historical hierarchical, exclusionary practices of the church that revers the senior male leader as the only viable voice and vessel for leadership. Even in some progressive churches that embrace women in ordained ministry, this hierarchal practice of ascribing parental authority over non-pastoral leaders within the church exists. This type of relational dynamic within team leadership does not align with the Biblical image of shared leadership modeled throughout scripture.

It is acknowledged that in 1st Timothy 1:18, Paul addresses Timothy as "my true son in the faith." However, that statement is based on the personal relationship Paul established with Timothy. Acts 16:1 speaks of the first encounter Paul has with Timothy, who is described as the son of a Jewish woman, who is a believer and a father, who was Greek (indicating non-believer). One can reasonably assume that Paul, as a Christian male role model, developed a paternal relationship with young Timothy as they worked intimately together in ministry. In examining the rest of Paul's letters, there is no evidence Paul intended this one reference to sonship to supersede all other relational examples of co-laboring (1 Corinthians 3:1-9) or shared leadership (Eph. 4:11-12) models. Maintaining the right perspective of others in team leadership as co-laborers who share in leading the church is essential for empowering everyone to be responsible for maintaining unity without regard for position, spiritual gifting, Divine call, or task responsibility.

To that end, Paul engages members of the leadership team to address the conflict between these two leaders with an appeal to help these women reconcile. Paul writes,

> "Yes, and I ask you also, my loyal companion, help these women for they have struggled beside me in the work of the gospel, together with Clement and the rest of my co-workers, whose names are in the book of life" (Phil. 4:3).

Paul, as a pastoral representative to this team of leaders in Philippi, became intimately involved when conflict arose, and he directed the other leaders at Philippi to do the same. Unfortunately, even Christian leaders can be conflict avoidant. However, it is a dereliction of duty for those called to 'maintain unity at all costs' to be afraid of engaging in conflict resolution within the team and the church at large. Together, leaders must have the emotional, spiritual, and relational ability, and willingness to engage one another toward reconciliation for the sake of unity.

Leadership Team Strategy for Maintaining Unity

Stay Focused

Paul lays out a strategy for the leadership team to follow to combat conflict when it occurs. Paul understands that what a person or team focuses on shapes the behavior of the person or team. To that end, Paul reminds them that the call to leadership is a call to oneness of mind in Christ. When Paul calls Euodia and Syntyche to be of one mind, he is referring to Philippians 2:1-5 where he writes:

> "[B]e of the same mind, having the same love, being in full accord and of one mind. Do nothing from selfish ambition or conceit, but in humility regard others as better than yourselves."

This appeal is a call to love and unity that strikes at the heart of a conflict that is usually a battle to be right. The fight to be right is a barrier to love. Paul's approach to unifying love begins with the mind and challenges how we choose to perceive others and ourselves. Leaders are expected to be open to compromise in conflict resolution that allows love and unity to remain.

Stay Positive

Paul also challenges the leadership team to maintain a positive perspective in their service to the Lord Jesus Christ. He exhorts the leaders at Philippi to remember to celebrate in the Lord always (Phil. 4:4). This is an interesting concept to consider for team leadership, especially when one recognizes the role leaders play in problem-solving. It is easy to rejoice when things go great, but what about when things are difficult, or the ministry has faced a major failure? The tendency is to focus on the negative and find fault and cast blame (whether spoken or unspoken). But what would team leadership look and feel like if the team agreed to celebrate everything in the Lord? The language would change. The atmosphere of team leadership would be more positive. Problems and conflicts would be viewed as opportunities for growth and transformation versus annoyances to avoid. For example, what if the children's ministry leader reports, "We lost oversight of a child today, and a member found him crossing the street." The response ought to be, "Praise God the child was found and was not harmed. Praise God, the member was responsive and got the child to safety. Praise God, we have been given an opportunity to improve our administrative processes and training volunteers." When the leadership team practices rejoicing in the Lord, the environment invites transformative change and influences ministry workers and the congregation to do the same. The result is a practice of faith that expects and celebrates the presence of God engaged in the life of the congregation. The leadership team that holds to this spiritual truth, no matter what the circumstances, looks to praise as the appropriate response.

Stay Humble

Paul recognizes the maturity of a leader's personality has a direct impact on the leader's ability to handle conflict well. Personality is defined here as the visible aspect of one's character as it impresses others, the sum total of the physical, mental, emotional, and social characteristics of an individual.[71]

Paul challenges the entire team to grow in Christian character when he declares, "Let your gentleness be known to everyone." (Phil. 4:5) Paul uses the Greek word for gentleness, *epieikes,* meaning "to be appropriately moderate, patient; to be one who is yielding and gives way to others."[72] Ephesians 4:2 makes reference to the same idea when Paul says, "With all humility and gentleness, with patience, bearing with one another in love." The leadership characteristics of gentleness and humility go hand in hand to balance the weight of leadership

---

[71] Dictionary.com, accessed July 28, 2017, http://www.dictionary.com/browse/personality.

[72] James Strong, *The New Strong's Exhaustive Concordance of the Bible* (Nashville, TN: Nelson Thomas Publishers, 1990), 31.

authority and responsibility. Paul recognizes leadership comes with a great deal of power and influence. The words and actions of leadership have intrinsic power that have very little to do with the person in the position. Those who have chosen to follow leadership ascribe this power to the leader. The leader must then do the intentional work of being gentle as an active practice of mature leadership. Paul goes on to remind the leaders that "[t]he Lord is near" (Phil. 4:5b), which is intended to humble the leader and remind him or her that they serve as ambassadors of Jesus Christ and not as agents of one's own objectives. Humbling one's self is what the leader does internally in order for gentleness to be experienced externally by others. This requires attending to one's spiritual and emotional center to maintain a posture of maturity within the leadership team.

Stay Prayerful

Paul goes on to address anxiety as a contributor to conflict. He says, "Do not worry about anything, but in everything by prayer and supplication with thanksgiving, let your request be known to God." (Phil. 4:6) Paul places prayer and faithful dependence on God in the toolkit for combating team anxiety that leads to conflict. Often this text is applied as an individual mandate, but here the context suggests that it is a shared leadership spiritual practice. The role of prayer in team leadership produces a unifying effect when everyone is praying about the same thing and seeking and gratefully expecting God to answer the team. This dependence on Divine intervention and instruction allows the team to move harmoniously through the practice of ministry, especially in difficult times. It suggests that team members should trust and depend on the shared spiritual relationship each teammate has with Jesus Christ. Prayer and faith provide a means for the team to slow down in order to consult God when clarity is needed, or conflicts arise. Anxiety is overcome when the team maintains a commitment to seek direction through group prayer. The result for the team is "the peace of God, which surpasses all understanding, will guard [the] hearts and [the] minds [of the leadership team] in Christ Jesus." (Phil. 4:7) Paul uses the Greek word for peace, *eirene,* from the primary verb *eiro,* meaning to join. Peace joins, so by definition, it is antithetical to the disunity anxiety produces. Peace is the result of being restored to oneness, quietness and rest.[73]

The pursuit of the peace of God through team prayer and thanksgiving is what joins the leadership team together and guards their hearts and minds to remain unified in Jesus Christ.

Stay Unity-minded

Lastly, Paul establishes a leadership team value statement 'that reminds the leaders of the top priorities, goals, and core beliefs of maintaining unified shared leadership."[74] He writes,

> Finally, beloved, whatever is true, whatever is honorable, whatever is pleasing, whatever is commendable, if there is any excellence and if there is anything worthy of praise,

---

[73] James Strong, 25.

[74] Business Dictionary 2017, BusinessDictionary.com, accessed July 28, 2017, http://www.businessdictionary.com/definition/value-statement.html

think about these things. Keep on doing the things that you have learned and received and heard and seen in me, and the God of peace will be with you." (Phil. 4: 8-9)

When the leadership team approaches every situation and interpersonal interaction from this vantage point, the redeemable value of each person on the team is the first consideration when disagreement occurs. Then the goal in conflict resolution becomes a process of restoration designed to move what isn't true to truth, what isn't honorable to honorable, what isn't pleasing to pleasing, what isn't commendable to commendable, what isn't excellent to excellence, what isn't worthy of praise to praiseworthy. This is the power of unity in team leadership. When conflict resolution is not an opportunity for personal attacks that result in disenfranchising team members by putting them at odds with one another or the group; but rather, the pursuit of unity is a means to practice heartfelt reconciliation as a unifying tool for the sake

of Jesus Christ

Final Reflections

The power of unity cannot be manufactured through special programming or measured through the number of members on the role or how many people sign on to the various online services now being offered. It is a way of being in relationship with one another that illustrates our connected faith in Jesus Christ. We have entered a new season in the life of the church. The coronavirus pandemic has disrupted our traditional ways of connecting with one another. The doors of the church building have closed (some forever) and have been replaced with Zoom meetings and pre-recorded worship services that limit the opportunities to personally interact with others. Protests calling for economic, health and policing justice for black and brown people has challenged long standing racial views across congregations and denominations of what is means "to act justly and to love mercy and to walk humbly with your God" and remain one body jointly knit together. But this isn't a time to shrink back and hope for things to return to the way the use to be. Now is the time to revisit and envision anew what the power of unity can look and feel like in practice in the midst of these challenges that have disrupted the status quo of the church universal.

Even as we consider the conflict that often exists in our individual congregations, I encourage all leadership teams to rethink how the power of unity can ignite the bonds of peace amongst your leadership and membership, help you stay connected through the Spirit of Jesus Christ without it being forced or rehearsed, and to remind each of us to nurture authentic community that is intentionally inclusive, relationally intimate and an authentic witness of unity experienced through love and grace that remains, even in the face of inevitable conflict.

BIBLIOGRAPHY

Berry, Erwin. *The Alban Personnel Handbook for Congregations.* Bethesda, MD: Alban Institute, 1999.

Dash, Michael J., and Christine D. Chapman. *The Shape of Zion: Leadership and Life in Black Churches.* Cleveland, OH: The Pilgrim Press, 2003.

Eguizabal, Orbelina, and Kevin E. Lawson. "Leading Ministry Teams, Part I: Theological Reflection on Ministry Teams." *Christian Education Journal* Series 3, 6, no. 2 (2009): 250-264.

Floyd-Thomas, Stacey, Juan Floyd-Thomas, Carol B. Duncan, and Nancy I. Westfield. *Black Church Studies: An Introduction.* Nashville, TN: Abingdon Press, 2007.

Ford, Kevin G. *Transforming Church: Bringing out the Good to Get to Great.* 2d ed. Colorado Springs, CO: David C. Cook Publishing Company, 2008.

Goleman, Daniel. "Leadership That Gets Results." *Harvard Business Review 78 - 90,* (March - April 2000) 20.

Goleman, Daniel, Richard Boyatzis, and Annie McKee. *Primal Leadership: Unleashing the Power of Emotional Intelligence.* Boston, MA: Harvard Business Review Press, 2013.

Heifetz, Ronald A., and Marty Linsky. *Leadership on the Line: Staying Alive through the Dangers of Leading.* Boston, MA: Harvard Business School Press, 2002.

Jones, Serene. "Graced Practices: Excellence and Freedom in Christian Life." In *Practicing Theology: Beliefs and Practices in Christian Life,* Edited by Miroslav Volf and Dorothy C. Bass, 51-77. Grand Rapids, MI: Wm. B. Eerdmans Publishing Co., 2002.

Kelly, J. N. D. *Early Christian Doctrines.* 5th ed. New York, NY: A&C Black, 1977.

LaFasto, Frank, and Carl Larson. *When Teams Work Best: 6,000 Team Members and Leaders Tell What It Takes to Succeed.* Thousand Oaks, CA: Sage Publications, Inc., 2001.

Larry, Kreider. *The Cry for Spiritual Fathers and Mothers.* Ephrata, PA: House to House Publishing, 2000.

Lawson, Kevin E., and Orbelina Eguizabal. "Leading Ministry Teams, Part II: Research on Effective Teams with Implications for Ministry Team Leadership." *Christian Education Journal* Series 3, 6, no. 2 (2009): 265-281.

Lencioni, Patrick. *The Five Dysfunctions of a Team: A Leadership Fable.* San Francisco, CA: Jossey-Bass, 2002.

Moltmann, Jurgen. *The Way of Jesus Christ.* Minneapolis, MN: Fortress Press, 1993.

Morse, Christopher. *Not Every Spirit: A Dogmatics of Christian Disbelief.* Harrisburg, PA: Trinity Press International, 1994.

Osborne, Larry. *Sticky Teams: Keeping Your Leadership Team and Staff on the Same Page.* Grand Rapids, MI: Zondervan, 2010.

Oshry, Barry. *Seeing Systems: Unlocking the Mysteries of Organizational Life.* 2d ed. San Francisco, CA: Berrett-Koehler Publishing, 2007.

Osmer, Richard R. *Practical Theology: An Introduction.* Grand Rapids, MI: Wm. B. Eerdmans Publishing Co., 2008.

Pauw, Amy Plantinga. "Attending to the Gaps Between Beliefs and Practices." In

Practicing Theology: Beliefs and Practices in Christian Life, Edited by Miroslav Volf and Dorothy C. Bass, 33-48. Grand Rapids, MI: Wm. B. Eerdmans Publishing Co., 2002.

Richardson, Ronald W. *Creating a Healthier Church: Family Systems, Leadership, and Congregational Life.* Minneapolis, MN: Fortress Press, 1996.

Sawyer, David. *The Work of the Church: Getting the Job Done in Boards and Committees.* 2d ed. Pressia, PA: Judson Press, 1987.

Strong, James. *The New Strong's Exhaustive Concordance of the Bible.* Nashville, TN: Nelson Thomas Publishers, 1990.

_____*Studying Congregations: A New Handbook.* Edited by Nancy T. Ammerman, Jackson W. Carroll, Carl S. Dudley, and William McKinney. Nashville, TN: Abingdon Press, 1998.

West, Cornel. *Race Matters.* Boston, MA: Beacon Press, 2007.

Willhauck, Susan, and Jacquelyn Thorpe. *The Web of Women's Leadership: Recasting Congregational Ministry.* Nashville, TN: Abingdon Press, 2001.